# House Training Your Puppy

## This Book Contains 2 Manuscripts:

## Crate Training Your Puppy

## Potty Training Your Puppy

### Kenneth Harrison

# Crate Training Your Puppy:

*Minimize Headaches and Accidents by Learning the Smartest Way to Train Your Puppy*

## Kenneth Harrison

# Table of Contents

Additionally, the information in the following pages is intended only for informational purposes and should thus be thought of as universal. As befitting its nature, it is presented without assurance regarding its prolonged validity or interim quality. Trademarks that are mentioned are done without written consent and can in no way be considered an endorsement from the trademark holder.

# Introduction

Crate training instills the appropriate behaviors in a puppy. For instance, if he has a habit of chewing on things, through crate training, your puppy will only have his toys to chew on and resist the urge of chewing on your household items.

Through crate training, a puppy will have his behavior modified. During travels, it can be extremely difficult to handle your puppy if he is not crated.

Keep in mind that for your puppy to take a liking to his crate, you must introduce it in an acceptable way. If you force him into the crate, he will resent being held in there, and the exercise will not bear any fruit.

A crate trained puppy allows the owner to be able to leave for work, knowing that their puppy is safe and secure. This book details everything you need to know about crate training so that your puppy can have a smooth time assimilating into your life.

# Chapter 1: The Basics of Crate training

Crate training is the process of introducing a crate to your dog and making them feel comfortable inside the crate. Most dog trainers consider it one of the most important tasks. Some of the reasons why people buy dog crates include:

- Toilet-training purposes
- Keeping your pet safe
- Establishing house rules
- Providing a place where your dog can feel at ease
- Acts as a unit for transporting your dog conveniently

Dogs love staying in dens. If you introduce the crate appropriately, your puppy will love it. Your puppy will run into it when they need to take a break from the house. In many instances, a puppy develops an attachment to their crate; they would even want to spend entire nights there.

Even if dogs are den-animals, if you take the wrong approach, they will resent the crates and possibly become scared of them. You need to exercise caution when crate training your dog.

## Introduce the crate carefully

Never come home one day with a crate and force your puppy inside it. It will scare them. Dogs resent being forced into any kind of situation that is against their will.

The best approach is to make the crate seem like a fun piece of furniture. Place it around a part of the house that they enjoy spending time in.

Make the interior well decorated and then stand back and watch whether they will be curious enough to go in. Do not forget to praise your dog every time that they walk into the crate.

Putting snacks and toys in the crate will encourage the dog to walk in. You can also initiate games with your dog around the crate so that they warm up to the idea of getting inside.

You want your dog to perceive the crate as a place for having fun and not a prison.

Gradually, start issuing subtle commands to your dog, like instructing them to go into the crate. Reward them whenever they obey. If your dog looks scared, stay until they are comfortable. Never walk out and assume that they will get used to it.

## Extend the stay

When the dog has gotten accustomed to climbing into the dog crate, the next challenge is to lengthen their stay. The intention is to create a positive notion about the crate, so that they may be able to stay in the crate for a long time without necessarily being checked on.

Setting up their meals inside the crate is a nifty way of ensuring a prolonged stay since the dog will eat and possibly take a nap, it will result in increasing their familiarity with the crate. Place the food towards the end of the crate, so that the dog will walk all the way in.

## Closing the crate

Once your dog has become somewhat accustomed to life in the crate, you should start closing it. This ensures that your dog can stay for a long period of time inside the cage without needing any attention.

Slamming the door shut while your dog is resting on their paunches is likely to scare them. The best approach is to shut the door slowly whenever the dog is busy with a toy or feeding.

Initially, when you close the door the dog might whine, you should open it again and try to soothe their anxiety away by gently stroking him and then slowly close it again. With careful approach and persistence, your dog should soon adjust to having the door of the crate closed.

Next, you can walk off to see how the dog copes with your absence, but stay nearby just in case they have separation anxiety. Calm down their fears and encourage them to withstand your absence. Soon, the dog will not only be comfortable in the cage but also will take a liking to it.

## Do not use the crate as a form of punishment

Some people tend to scoop their dog up when they have done a mistake and shove them into the crate. This causes the dog to develop negative feelings about the crate.

Moving on, it becomes hard to get your dog to ever want to be in the crate. If you want your dog to be happy about spending time in the crate, you should ensure that they have positive feelings about the crate.

## Space

Ensure that the crate is large enough for the dog to move around. Depending on the size of the dog, you want to buy a crate that can accommodate them reasonably well, but not too large at the same time.

## Safety

The crate might serve as your dog's haven when you are not around, and because of this, you want to ensure that the crate is as safe as could be. First off, ensure that there are no sharp edges, as they put your dog at risk of skin tear.

Ensure there are no spaces through which a predator could come in. Do not forget to take off the collar so that the dog may be free to move around.

# Chapter 2: Why Should You Crate Train Your Puppy?

Crate training has been termed as one of the most important things to do for your dog. Some dog owners seem uncomfortable with the whole idea, at least initially. Here are some of the reasons why crate training your dog is considered important.

## It is a safe haven

Dogs have it in their nature to stay in dens. When you consider the atmosphere of many homes, you can understand that from time to time your dog will need to pull away from all the activities and spend some alone time in a "den."

Having a dog crate serves this purpose. When your dog climbs into the crate, you should let them have some quality time on their own. This will lead to an emotionally gratified dog that will connect with you at an even deeper level. Also, the crate serves as a refuge to the dog whenever they face a threat.

## Housetraining purposes

Dog owners get frustrated when their dog relieves themselves without paying attention to where they are. Crates are vital equipment, as they help you teach your dog how to control their bladder and bowel movement.

When you housetrain your dog, you must exercise patience and resist from punishing your dog when they fail to adhere to your rules. The whole exercise must hinge on patience and persistence. In the end, your dog will become disciplined enough to relieve himself where you want them to. After all, dogs hate dwelling in a soiled environment.

## Safety

It can be nerve-wracking to go to work and leave your dog behind, imagining all the crazy things your dog might be up to. A dog crate provides a sanctuary for your dog.

This way, you can enclose the dog in the haven when you are not around. Also, when you are having a renovation in your house or cleaning it, you may keep the dog in the crate as it would be dangerous for them frolicking around, considering that sharp tools might harm them.

## Fun

When you get your dog a crate, one of the things you must provide is a toy. This will ensure that the dog will have something to play with as the hours roll by.

When your dog has some toys in their crate, they can easily chew on those toys instead of other valuable things in your household like furniture. Also, crates are great for feeding your dog. Ideally, you should put the food toward the end. When you combine food and attractive toys, your dog will be very entertained.

## Traveling

It can be quite hectic to move around when the dog is not restrained. For instance, it is convenient to have your dog in the crate when you are traveling by road, as opposed to them prancing around in the car, which would pose safety concerns.

A dog crate ensures that your dog is confined in a comfortable environment, in which they can function without facing constraints. The preparation encourages the dog to develop a positive feeling toward the crate so that eventually, they become attached to the crate and want to spend most of their time there.

## Guests

Not to mean that guests are allergic to dogs, but for some reason, you might prefer to have the dog held away when your guests are around. If you lack a dog crate, you will not be able to do it without hurting your dog's feelings. A crate serves as a good place to put your dog when you have guests over.

## Easier vet visits

Sometimes, the dog might come down with an illness that requires them to stay with the vet for more than a day. In such instances, it does the vet a world of good that the dog is crate trained. The dog will also be far more at peace in a new territory when they are confined in their crate.

## For calming your dog

Some dogs can really escalate their feelings and actions. In such cases, a significant amount of damage is done. A crate is crucial for managing such dogs. You may put your dog in the crate as a way of calming them down. A crate trained dog responds well to time-outs.

## Evacuation

As long as you live in a modern house, there are various potential disasters and emergencies. It is easier to evacuate a dog who has been crate trained than the one who is not. If your dog is handed over to new owners, the separation hurts them less because they are still in their own crate and surrounded by familiar items.

# Chapter 3: Picking the Best Crate for Your Dog

A dog crate gives your dog his own personal space. There are several things to consider before selecting a dog crate: how you plan to use it, the age of your dog, their personality, and their breed.

The practical concerns include: how easy it is to clean and carry around, and whether the color and material of the crate align with your aesthetic taste.

Dog crates come in a wide range of sizes, styles, designs, and materials. All dog crates will hold your dog and help with potty training.

Picking the dog crate that is best for you will depend on the size of your dog and other variables. Here are some of the questions that you should ask yourself before you purchase a crate:

- Will the crate get moved around or will it stay in one place?
- Will you travel long distances with the crate?
- Does your dog have the habit of chewing on things?
- Will it be easy to clean up this crate?
- How does the crate fit into your home and decor?

The biggest mistake that most dog owners make is buying a crate that is a few sizes too big. Before you buy a crate, you should first measure the size of your dog.

To get their height, you should measure from the top of their shoulders to their paws; to get their length, you should measure from the tip of their nose to the tip of their tail. The ideal crate should allow your dog to stand up, sit down, and turn around comfortably. The door should be wide enough for the dog to go in and out without any difficulties.

These are the five basic types of dog crates:

1. **Plastic crates**
2. **Wire crates**
3. **Heavy-duty crates**

4. **Soft-sided crates**
5. **Cute crates**

# 1. Plastic crates

It takes two pieces of molded plastic to make this type of crate. The top and bottom are held in place by plastic fasteners, and there is a metal-wire door.

Some crates designed for puppies tend to have a plastic door which is a huge drawback, considering that puppies like chewing on things. Most plastic crates have a moat that runs around the edge of the floor which traps the dog's urine and drains it.

## Advantages of plastic crates

- The space is comfortable
- Makes it easier to travel with your dog
- Good at containing puppies
- Available in different colors
- The top half can come off easily and get stacked with the bottom half for easier storage

## Disadvantages of plastic crates

- On warm days, it can get hot in there
- It limits your dog's scope of vision which might disorient them

- Not very aesthetically pleasing

## 2. Wire dog crates

For the most part, these crates are made of panels of wire, but the floor is made of plastic. The material that is used is sturdy, and it also discourages the habit of chewing up things.

### Advantages of wire crates

- It has great ventilation which allows dogs to be at ease. The wire crate is perhaps the best choice for dogs living in hot climates.
- You can section off the crate using a divider. This allows you to increase the area occupied by the dog as they grow older.
- It can be folded. This proves important when carrying or storing the crate.
- The removable floor makes it easy to clean.

### Disadvantages of wire crates

- They produce more noise than plastic crates when your dog moves around
- Some models are weak enough for a dog to break free.
- The design is not attractive

## 3. Soft-sided crates

Soft-sided is considered the most portable crates. It is available in a wide range of styles, sizes, and materials.

**Advantages of soft-sided crates**

- It is lightweight, which makes it easy to carry your dog around.
- Ideal for containing a dog with serious separation anxiety.
- The best for traveling and camping. Due to its lightweight status, you can bring your dog along for road travels and even camping.
- It is very easy to store since it can be folded.

**Disadvantages of soft-sided crates**

- Hard to clean up in case of a major potty accident.
- Some dogs can chew their way out.
- Some dogs might figure out how to open the zip door.

## 4. Heavy-duty crates

These crates are designed using heavy-duty material. They are available in various styles and colors.

**Advantages of heavy-duty crates**

- There is almost a zero chance that the dog will break free.

- They are the most suitable for traveling by air.

## Disadvantages of heavy-duty crates

- It is expensive, but keep in mind that they are made of sturdy material which justifies the expense.

## 5. Cute crates

As the name suggests, the cute crates are aesthetically pleasing, compared to the rest. They are mostly made of wood and exotic materials.

## Advantages of cute crates

- It has a tasteful design.
- It is designed for comfort.

## Disadvantages of cute crates

- Destructive dogs can chew at the wood

# Chapter 4: The Importance of Exercise When Crate Training Your Puppy

Just like humans, dogs benefit from exercising as well. There are various exercises you may incorporate in your training regimen to strengthen your dog. Here are some of the benefits of putting your dog through exercises.

- **Bone health**

  When your dog does exercises like walking around, the muscles around his tendons will become strong. This improves his bone health and helps keep diseases at bay.

- **Heart health**

  Regular exercises will strengthen his heart. Exercising will increase the oxygen demands of his body, making his lungs more active. This will lead to optimal functioning lungs and heart, to keep up with the demands of his body. When he is constantly active, it minimizes the risk of developing heart complications.

- **Minimizes aggression**

  One of the many reasons why dogs may act aggressively is because they have pent-up energy. When they engage in various exercises, it is actually a way of letting go of the aggression, nervousness, and anxiety. They will be much more welcoming to strangers and critters.

- **Fights boredom**

  When your dog is bored, he is going to try to get your attention by whining and doing other things that you probably warned him against. However, he will feel entertained when you make him perform some exercises. When he is entertained, he is less likely to disturb you with whining or barking.

- **Improves metabolism**

Naturally, the metabolism of a dog can cater to some heavy-duty activities. When you make him perform exercises, you are actually enhancing the optimal function of his body. Exercising will enhance his metabolism rate.

- **Improves sleep**

  It is no secret that dogs love sleeping, but it can be hard for your dog to get quality sleep if he has been inactive throughout the day. When you make him perform some exercises, you will tire him out, and he will be able to get quality sleep. When a dog gets quality sleep, it helps his attitude. He becomes less aggressive and more receptive to the instructions of his owner.

- **Controls weight**

  The exercises help your dog burn calories which contribute to managing his weight. If your dog just consumes food and lies around, you can expect that he will gain weight. Gaining unnecessary weight could give rise to various health complications like heart disease.

- **Reduces separation anxiety**

Some dogs tend to develop a great bond with their owner, that they cannot ever withstand being separated. Exercising is one method of reducing the level of attachment that the dog has for his owner.

When you take him around for walks before you leave for work, it will trigger feelings of happiness in him, making him less inclined to whine or bark when you finally leave for work. Exercises will also tire him out and leave him wanting to sleep, making it easier for him to let you go to work.

- **Reduced chewing**
  Puppies are especially guilty of this habit. A puppy that is going through the teething phase tends to examine things with his mouth.

  Puppies have an overwhelming urge to chew at things. When you notice him doing it, you have to warn him that it is an inappropriate behavior.

  Warning him alone is not enough; the puppy will always get around to chewing more of your things. If you start putting him through routine exercises, his tendency of chewing at things will eventually fade away. The exercises will refresh him and make him calm.

- **Eliminate predatory behavior**
Your canine friend can have some serious predatory behaviors, which can make him harmful to either kids or critters. This is partly due to boredom and the pursuit of drama.

  He could become hostile toward other people, and you would find yourself having to confine him and keep him away when guests come over. Exercising will make him spend his pent-up energy and put him in a good mood. He will be less inclined to treat others with hostility.

- **Increased agility**
Dogs naturally have to be agile to perform their activities. Since your puppy does not live in his natural habitat, you will have to devise ways of making him agile. Adding exercise to his routine is the most obvious way of ensuring that he is agile. You have to incorporate fun into the exercises and make them varied.

- **Prevents premature aging**

As an animal age, their lean muscle tends to diminish. If your dog just eats and sits around, he is likely to age at a faster rate compared to him being engaged in some exercises. A combination of good nutrition and routine exercises will promote the growth of lean muscle.

- **Get rid of toxins**

   When your puppy is inactive, he is at risk of accumulating toxic elements in his body. A sedentary lifestyle encourages harmful elements to build up inside his body. If he exercises, his body will function at an optimum level, which will lead to the elimination of toxic substances.

# Chapter 5: What to do When Your Puppy is whining in the Crate

A puppy communicates his needs through cries, just like an infant. When you put your puppy in a crate, he will express his discomfort by crying, and it could take days for him to adjust to the new environment.

Whenever your puppy whines, be careful how you handle him because your response could affect his future behaviors. Here are some of the reasons that drive your puppy into whining and how to make him stop.

- **Sickness**

When your puppy whines all the time, it could be an indication that he is physically or emotionally unwell. Some of the symptoms to look out for include loss of appetite, diarrhea, lethargy, dizziness, vomiting, and shortness of breath.

If the puppy has bitten, licked, or scratched himself excessively around a certain area of his body, it is indicative of an infection, allergy, parasitic attack, and other skin issues.

If your puppy becomes withdrawn and recoils when you touch him, it is a sign that he is in a world of physical and emotional pain. When you discover any of these symptoms, you should take him to a vet for medical attention.

- **Loneliness**
  The puppy may be struggling with the separation from his parents. This results to whining as a way of sending out an alarm in case the mother can hear him and come to his rescue.

  When you are dealing with an emotionally hurting puppy, the whining is usually low-pitched and never-ending. The best way to make him stop is to comfort him by making him see you a lot more. You can carry off the crate to a part of your house where you may interact with him while you are engaged in other things.

- **Fear**

  Various things about the new environment could trigger fear in your puppy. This will make your puppy whine. Inspect the crate and ensure there is nothing wrong. Also, reassure the puppy that everything is alright by stroking him and giving him treats.

- **Hunger**

  Your puppy could also whine due to hunger. Once you give him something to feed on, and he runs to the food like a rat to cheese, then you can be sure that it is hunger. If he ignores the food, it could mean something else is the cause of his discomfort.

- **Boredom**

  Another reason why the puppy could whine is due to boredom. Puppies love having a partner to play with to expend their energy. In the absence of a partner, toys will do. Get them a toy that piques their interest, and they will turn to it to fight the boredom away.

Here are more tips to make your puppy stop crying when you are not sure what the crying is all about:

- **Take him to the potty**

  Perhaps your puppy wants to relieve himself and is trying to get your attention. If he whines in the crate, carry him off to the potty. As soon as he relieves himself, carry him back into his crate without any distractions.

- **Play with him**

  Try to play with him and see how he reacts. This is likely going to get him into a good mood. Playing for a long duration will tire him out and make him want to sleep, which will put an end to his whining.

- **Put a sheet over the wire crate**

  In as much as wire crates are great for ventilation purposes, they are uncomfortable to a certain extent, especially during the night. Spreading a sheet over the wire crate will make your puppy feel more at ease, but you have to be careful in how you tuck away the ends because some puppies will not mind chewing at the sheet.

- **Bring the crate to your room**

If all your attempts to make him stop crying bear no fruits, you might as well consider bringing the crate into your room. This is certainly going to make him stop whining, especially when he is enveloped by your scent.

- **Discourage whining**
  A puppy is at an impressionable stage. You can use psychological tricks to modify his behavior.

  First of all, when he whines, make him stop and then praise him for not whining. You may give him treats and stroke him gently for not whining.

  Stop praising him and turn away when he whines. This will condition him to believe that he will only receive praise when he is not whining. Since he is at an impressionable stage, he will want to please you by doing what appears to make you happy.

# Here are the two things not to do when your dog whines:

- Do not shout at him. In the worst case scenario, your puppy could misinterpret this as hostility and become scared. On the other hand, he could also perceive this as interest on your part and carry on with the whining, under the illusion that you are enjoying this activity too.

- Do not use a shock collar. A shock collar is a terrible way of making your dog stop whining. It could hurt him and make him resent being held in the crate.

# Chapter 6: How to Handle Separation Anxiety When Crate Training Your Puppy

Dogs crave for their owner's attention. They hate it when their owner leaves them alone. For instance, when you leave for work your dog will probably make you feel guilty to look at you with pitiful eyes. Some other dogs will react more aggressively.

Dogs suffering from extreme separation anxiety will bark endlessly, try to ruin everything in their path, and relieve themselves around the house. In some cases, they may even injure themselves as they try to escape.

First of all, you have to establish whether your dog is suffering from separation anxiety or if he is just bored. When your dog is not getting stimulated enough, he can easily get bored and will resort to entertaining himself through barking and chewing at things.

You also have to find out whether your dog is exhibiting true separation anxiety or just 'learned' separation anxiety. Learned separation anxiety is caused by low self-control, and the behaviors that he exhibits are merely simulated. However, when a dog experiences true separation anxiety, he gets stressed whenever his owner is absent.

## Signs of separation anxiety:

- Dedicating himself to destroying things
- Trying to get away from home while you are absent
- Relieving himself around the house even though he is potty trained
- Wearing pitiful eyes when you are about to leave the house
- Howling and barking during the day
- Purposely inflicting self-harm
- Acting clingy
- Barking and jumping when you finally come back home

## Stop making a big deal out of leaving or arriving at home

Dog owners unknowingly trigger separation anxiety when they make a big deal of leaving or arriving home. Now, this makes your dog more conscious of your absence.

Ceremonial departures and arrivals can affect your dog's capacity to withstand your absence. When you have to leave for work in the morning, resist making a loud gesture that announces your intent to leave like grabbing car keys theatrically. When you come back, do not rush to pet him.

## The power of exercise

Your dog has a lot of energy, and when he lacks a creative way of spending it, he might resort to raising hell and chewing at things. One of the best ways of spending your dog's energy is to take him out for a walk before you leave.

This exercise will relieve his anxiety and improve his mood and finally when you leave he will be too tired to complain. Introduce new challenges during the walk and make it as eventful as possible.

## Leave behind a personal item with your puppy

Dogs have a strong sense of smell. They recognize your smell. When you leave behind a personal item of yours, the scent will remind your puppy of you. It will help comfort him whenever he feels unsafe. You may opt to leave behind a blanket or pillow.

## The charm of toys

Nothing excites a puppy more than playtime. You could get him a puzzle toy to play with throughout the day.

Before you leave, give him a toy that challenges his skills. He will focus on the toy and have less time to mourn your departure.

Toys provide an escape from boredom as they cater to your puppy's need for stimulation. You might want to buy various puzzle toys to keep your puppy from getting bored.

Give him a different set of toys every day. Your departure will still be a bitter pill to swallow, but it will signify the start of games.

## Be consistent

It can be difficult to establish a routine, especially where puppies are concerned, but it is a sure way of handling separation anxiety. When a dog settles into a routine, he is far less affected by your absence. Make him anticipate walking, feeding, playing and sleeping.

## Take him to a daycare

Daycares are great for the social development of your dog. Find out a convenient daycare around your area of residence, and take him there. Track his development. Keep in mind that some dogs are terrified of populated areas.

## Contact a dog behaviorist

If your dog is battling an extreme separation anxiety, consider taking him to a dog behaviorist and trainer. Tell him about your dog's tendencies and explore the various solutions available.

# Chapter 7: What to do When Accidents Occur

The important thing is that you do not harm your dog. If you harm your dog because of an accident, he will associate the act with a negative feeling and next time he might do it at a more secluded area, where he thinks that you cannot find out.

## Cleaning Urine

- **Paper towels**

  First, you ought to dry off the urine. A bunch of paper towels is great for wiping off the urine. With a gloved hand, press a bunch of paper towels or a rag onto the urine and clean the surface. If you have no gloves, you could use your foot, and this shields you against germs.

- **Carpet cleaner**

  Using paper towels are not enough, as the urine would dry off and there would be a conspicuous stain. Spray carpet cleaner on the urinated spot and wait for a few minutes to pass, then spray the carpet cleaner a second time and wipe the surface again. This will ensure that a stain will not develop afterward.

- **Baking soda**

  The urine of the dog harbors various germs. Baking soda is one of the most common household disinfectants. Sprinkle a generous amount of the baking soda over the spot and wipe it off. The baking soda not only destroys the activity of germs but also gets rid of the smell of the dog urine.

## Cleaning Waste

Though it is common for a dog to urinate or waste separately, in some instances, he might both urinate and waste at the same time. Cleaning waste tends to be slightly more difficult.

- **Pick up the waste**
  Put gloves in your hands. Then hold open an inside-out grocery bag.

  Using a bunch of paper towels, grab as much waste off of the floor and put it in the inside-out grocery bag. When you are done collecting the waste, spray the floor with carpet cleaner to ensure that the waste does not dry off and give the room a terrible smell.

  Wipe the spray off the floor and sprinkle a generous amount of baking soda after a few minutes. The waste contains an army of germs. The baking soda is crucial in disinfecting your home surface as well as neutralizing the smell of the dog waste.

## Tips on preventing accidents

Every dog owner has dealt with these kinds of accident. No matter how careful you are, your canine friend is going to surprise you from time to time. When an accident happens, you must act appropriately, so as not to you affect his future behavior.

## Ensure that no medical issues are dogging him

Ensure that there are no medical issues that are limiting his capacity to control himself. When several accidents occur in a short amount of time, consider taking him to a vet office for a thorough health examination.

Some of the medical issues that trigger accidents include diarrhea, urinary tract infection, kidney stones, and bladder complications.

## Interrupting his business

Dogs are very cunning, and when they have to relieve themselves, they crave some level of privacy. In most cases, you will be too late to remedy the situation.

However, there are some instances when you catch him in the middle of relieving himself or just before. In such instances, you have to intersect and lead him off to the appropriate spot.

## Take him out more

When you make a habit of taking him out frequently, he will have more opportunity to relieve himself in the designated area. Depending on his age and breed, you can adjust the gaps between the breaks.

Make the effort of coming along instead of ordering him to go out alone. And when he displays appropriate potty manners, do not forget to praise him.

Puppies love to please their master, and when they associate their potty manners with making their master glad, they will be more inclined to upholding their potty manners. Track his progress and try to establish whether there is a pattern to his accidents.

**Utilize the crate**

It can be a bit tricky to ensure that there are no accidents while you are not watching. When you are sure that he is not going to relieve himself, you can let him wander through the house.

However, if he is going to be unattended for a long period of time, it is practical to confine him in a crate. Although, be sure not to confine him for much longer than he can handle.

**Become more present**

For the most part, an accident never occurs on willful commission. If there is no underlying medical issue, the accident may be as a result of a lapse in leadership. Your dog does not have a big brain. He has to be guided patiently and persistently until the system feels natural to him.

# Chapter 8: Putting It Altogether – Creating a Crate training Plan that Works

Dogs have a natural denning instinct. Dog trainers advocate for crate training dogs so that they may have a safe and secure place to spend time and sleep, just as it would have been their natural setting.

Puppies need to be constantly watched. If they are left on their own, they will probably destroy valuable items and even endanger their lives. Since the dog owner is unlikely to have the whole day to spend with his puppy, the only viable option is to crate him.

With the right approach, you can introduce the crate to your puppy and make him appreciate being held in there. However, if you do not train him well he might despise the crate and attach negative feelings to the experience of being crated.

It is critical to crate your puppy because some of the benefits include:

- **Faster housetraining**
  A crate trained puppy takes well to housetraining. It can be distressing to have a puppy with bad potty manners, but crate training him will improve his capacity to control his bladder and bowel movement.

- **Protecting both him and your belongings**
  There are a lot of materials in your house that are potential health hazards to your puppy. You will be exposing him to these hazards when you let him roam around without your supervision.

  For instance, he could jump around and end up knocking down an object that may hurt him. Puppies love chewing at things. When you let him roam your house unattended, he will find a lot of items to chew on, thus ruining your belongings and not to mention that it may subject him to intestinal problems.

- **Comfort**
Dogs love having a place of their own that they can retreat to when they want to be alone. The normal day can involve a lot of games, and he will eventually need to take a break from all the games and retreat to his improvised "cave." Whenever he feels threatened, he may run into his crate, and he will even spend the nights there as well.

- **Managing problems**
Untrained puppies exhibit behaviors that are generally improper. It is upon the dog owner to show his puppy the acceptable way of behaving. Crate training your dog goes a long way in instilling healthy habits and by modifying his behaviors further. For instance, he will learn to answer your calls, rather than ignoring your commands.

- **Travel**
Considering the hassles of traveling, it would be unwise to carry your puppy around. If you are traveling by road, it could pose various risks to him.

If you are traveling by air, authorities require that you use a crate. When you have your puppy confined in a crate, it becomes so much easier to handle him during travels.

When you buy the crate, ensure that it will meet the needs of your puppy. Consider the model and material of the crate that you buy, but above everything else, the crate should be just the right size to allow him to stand, sit down and turn around comfortably.

## Introducing the crate

Never hold your puppy by the scruff of his neck and shove him into the crate. He will loathe every second he is held inside.

You have to figure out how to introduce the crate in a way that he will take a liking to it. First off, bribe him with treats and toys.

When you put a treat or a chewable toy inside, it will be enough incentive for your puppy to scurry into the crate. Leave the door open to show him that he can step out if he wants to.

Gradually, put the treats and the toys toward the farthest end so that he will have to walk all the way in. When he gets used to climbing into the crate, you can start closing the door and leaving him.

Start leaving him inside gradually, first for short moments and then for a prolonged amount of time. You have to come back from time to time to check on how he is doing, particularly to take him out so that he may relieve himself.

When a crate is properly used, the benefits are immense. However, some puppies can never cope with the fright of being contained in a crate and having their owner move away.

Such puppies should not be crated. Other instances when you should not hold your puppy in a crate include:

- **Escape attempts**
  If your puppy damages his crate in an attempt to escape, it is time to replace it or have it repaired.
- **Dampness**
  If the floor of the crate is damp, resist using that crate. The dampness is mostly caused by excessive salivation.
- **Accidents**
  When your dog defecates or urinates in the crate, you have to stop using it, at least until it is cleaned. Dogs have repetitive behaviors, and that

means they will be inclined to defecate on the spot that they previously defecated on.

- **Weather**

   Puppies get scared too easily. When the weather is terribly bad, you want to offer him reassurance. Have him stay close to you, instead of being on his own in his crate.

# Chapter 9: Housetraining Using Crates

The purpose of housetraining is to instill discipline in your puppy and develop a close bond with him. To achieve the best results, you have to be persistent, patient and have a good attitude.

The amount of time needed to housetrain your puppy depends on some factors, but it takes from about a few months to a whole year for a puppy to be fully housetrained.

## Begin early

Dog trainers suggest that you should begin to housetrain your puppy as soon as he is 12 weeks old. His ability to control his bladder and bowel movement begins to take shape around that age.

## Get a crate

Puppies do not like soiling their private space. You have to get him a crate that fits his size, or else he is going to convert one side of the crate into his bathroom.

Teach him slowly that he must walk out to relieve himself. The best crate for him will depend on some internal and external factors. For instance, if it is very hot, you have to get him a crate that is ventilated.

## Feeding schedule

Puppies love routines. When it comes to feeding, put him on a routine so that he is aware of his feeding time, and so that you may be able to distinguish his cycle of relieving himself. When it is not feeding time, take away the food. This will increase his level of self-control.

## Pick a potty spot

Your puppy will be less inclined to soiling his crate if you provide a place where he will feel comfortable relieving himself. For instance, you could train him to relieve himself on a small area of your yard.

It becomes easy to build up on that behavior because puppies like relieving themselves on the exact same area they did before. This does not mean that you have automatically eradicated all possibility of an accident.

With patience and persistence, you can make his potty manners excellent.

## Taking him out

One thing you have to understand about puppies is that they adore being guided by the owner. Until they are trained properly, they cannot take initiative.

You will have to take him out for the most part of housetraining. In the morning, the first thing is to check up on the little guy, and take him out to relieve himself.

During the day, you can start taking him out at 30-minute intervals, and then increase it to an hour. When he clears a meal, wait for a short moment and then take him out.

You should also take him out every time he wakes up from a nap. Before you put him back in his sleeping abode at night, ensure that he relieves himself.

## Praise him

Puppies are very sensitive and are always in need of their owner's attention. There is no better way of showering him with attention, than a reward for his good deeds.

For instance, when he exhibits excellent potty manners, praise him. He is going to want to keep up his manners so that he can please you, and earn praise from you in return. Also, it will foster a great bonding experience when you praise him.

## Set up an area for playing

Younger puppies require to be taken out more frequently than older ones. You should never keep your puppy confined in his crate for more than six hours during the day.

You can ask someone else to take them out if you are not around or you may want to drop them off at a daycare. If that is not entirely possible, you have to create a place where he will be free to play.

Place everything he requires around that playing area and leave him alone with the knowledge that his mess will be easy to clean up, as it will be restricted to that area alone.

## Learn the signs

Puppies cannot express their needs like a human being, but there are still cues to watch out for to inform you what he wants. When he is not feeling good, he will display behaviors such as whining, barking, circling, and sniffing. You have to go and take him out.

## Puppies get scared

When you take him out to relieve himself at night, hang around until he actually does it. Puppies are very sensitive and have a tendency of getting scared especially if the weather is bad.

When they are scared, it limits their capacity to relieve themselves. You will want to offer him security and make sure that he is relieving himself.

Some people who leave their puppy alone outside often find that the puppy ends up relieving himself inside the house instead. He was probably too scared to do it outside.

The key to housetraining a puppy is supervision. If you are too busy to supervise him, you have to consider getting help.

# Chapter 10: Feeding Your Dog in the Crate

Devising a great diet plan for your puppy is a big task. Dog trainers warn against creating variety because it could harm his digestion.

You have to throw any leftover food and ensure that the bowls have water throughout the day. The diet requirements for puppies are much more intense than the requirements for older dogs because puppies are physically developing at a massive rate.

To come up with a perfect diet plan, you have to conduct your research and even seek help from the breeder.

# First-year timeline

- **6 – 12 weeks**

  Puppy food is all their bodies can withstand. If you give them adult food, it could harm their vulnerable digestive system, not to mention that there would probably be a case of nutrition deficiency. Ideally, the puppy should be fed around four times each day.

- **3 – 6 months**

  At this stage, the puppy's body is taking shape, and you may slightly reduce the amount of food.

- **6 – 12 months**

  Gradually make the switch from puppy food into adult food. You can feed him twice a day.

# Dry foods

There is a wide selection of dry foods in the market. You have to buy the food that is tailored for your puppy.

The best food for your puppy depends on various factors like the key ingredients it contains, and the price it costs. However, the most expensive dry foods contain the highest concentration of nutrients.

# Semi-moist and tinned foods

The quality depends on the price range. But you have to stick with ingredients that work for your puppy. Buy complete foods as opposed to foods that require you to make additions.

## Treats

The best treats should have a great taste and at the same time, cater to a dog's dietary needs. Treats should be given economically. Some treats may contain lots of milk products, sugar, colorings, fat and even chemicals, so you have to find treats that will not affect your puppy.

## Selecting high-quality puppy food

Your puppy's nutrition needs are high. Before you purchase any foods, you first have to do your research and analyze the foods carefully. You can solicit advice from vet officers and the breeder.

And when you introduce a type of food to your puppy, always study how your puppy reacts. If he appears allergic to it, you have to stop giving him more of that food.

## How to determine whether the puppy food will meet your puppy's needs

The nutritional guidelines that most pet food manufacturers follow are set by the American Feed Control Officials. Always check if the package label states that the food is AAFCO-compliant. The label should also indicate the stage of the puppy that the food is meant for.

## How much should you feed your puppy?

Puppies are in a state of rapid growth in their first five months. To keep up with their caloric demands, you should serve them a generous amount of food. You can be guided by the feeding charts on product labels. They recommend appropriate amounts of food basing on the age and weight of the puppy.

## Knowing whether your puppy is feeding well

Vet officers examine the state of a puppy using the body conditioning score, which ranges from one to five, with one standing for emaciated, and five standing for obesity. A healthy puppy should clock two.

## What kind of foods can harm your puppy?

Some of the foods that people eat can have harmful effects on your puppy. These foods include raisins, grapes, avocados, macadamia, bread, garlic, onion, dairy products, coffee, alcohol, gum, and candy.

## Puppy feeding tips

- **Understand the nutritional content**
  Always examine the nutritional value of the dog food.
  Some ingredients may be doing more harm than good
  to your dog. To be clear about the appropriate
  ingredients, you may want to seek guidance from the
  breeder.

- **Do not feed him the moment you come home**
  Feeding him as soon as you arrive will trigger an
  emotional message and encourage attachment.
  Therefore, his separation anxiety will increase.

  Arrange for him to be fed on a schedule. If you arrive
  with a fanfare, you are going to make him emotional,
  and he will not be okay with you leaving him again.

  Instead, when you arrive home, you may want to do
  some other activity first before you come back to him,
  but if you must attend to him first, it should be
  nothing more than petting and playing around.

- **Consult a vet officer before changing your
  puppy's diet**

Putting your puppy under a variety of diets will give rise to digestion complications. Consult your veterinary officer and also the breeder if you have to change your puppy's diet.

- **Create the right environment for having meals**
  Never try to take away your puppy's food while he is eating. This could trigger his food aggression and complicate his overall behavior.

- **Meal timing**
  Do not feed your puppy before he travels by car. Otherwise, he will experience car sickness. Also, do not feed him shortly before or after exercising as this would lead to bloating.

- **Do not encourage begging**
  Never feed your dog from the table, as this will encourage him to start seeking your attention through begging.

- **Plenty of water**
  Puppies have a serious need for water. You should station bowls of clean water in their crates and also at strategic positions around their playing area.

Their water consumption goes up during the summer. You should consider increasing the number of bowls.

# Chapter 11: Steps to Prevent Whining and Barking

Barking and whining are the two common ways that your dog communicates his needs, but it can be irritating when your dog barks or whines nonstop. The key towards preventing your dog from barking himself hoarse is to ensure that you have eliminated all scenarios that would encourage barking.

Here are some of the tips for preventing your dog from whining and barking:

## Check on him regularly

Puppies are in need of constant attention. If you go for a long time without checking up on him, you risk making him relieve himself where he should not, as well as whine and bark incessantly.

You should especially keep an eye on him if you know that he is recently fed. Realize that puppies do not have a lot of control over their bladders or bowel movement and they will relieve themselves at the slightest inclination.

When you check up on him regularly, it will be easy to find out his needs, and make him comfortable. You are also able to guide him to the appropriate location to relieve himself.

If he is the type that gets scared easily, your constant presence will help him adjust to the environment and will get rid of his anxiety.

## Get the appropriate crate size

What is the appropriate crate size? One that allows him to stand, sit down, turn around, and get through the door without a hassle.

Most dog owners make the mistake of buying a crate that is a few sizes too big. If you are going to leave him inside the crate for a prolonged period of time, understand that he will walk up to one side of the crate and relieve himself.

A crate is not the best place for relieving himself. Dogs hate sleeping in an area that has been soiled.

The excrement will attract all sorts of bad bacteria, which will harm your dog. Under such circumstances, your dog will develop an inclination towards barking and whining.

When you acquire the right size of a crate, it will encourage him to develop appropriate potty manners, therefore, keeping his abode safe and clean.

## Take him for bathroom breaks regularly

Your dog does not have a mouth to speak for himself. You will have to train him so that he may get along with you.

When you make him overstay behind closed doors, you are only asking that he relieves himself there. Get into the habit of taking him to his potty.
When he relieves himself appropriately, praise him verbally and give him a treat. He will associate proper potty manners with receiving a treat.

This will eliminate chances of accidents, as well as stabilize your dog's emotional state so that he will refrain from barking and whining.

## Eliminate distractions

Dogs have very developed senses. They can perceive things and people long before you do.

For instance, a dog might become aware of an approaching person long before you will, and resort to barking. It could seem like he is barking for no reason at all until the person gets into your line of sight.

When you eliminate distractions, you will create an enabling environment for your dog to relax, and focus on his activities. You have to be especially careful where you position his crate.

Ideally, you should place the crate in an open and quiet area. If there are distractions, like kids playing, the dog is likely to respond with incessant barking.

It does not necessarily mean that he is scared. He might be making a cry of glee and is probably asking to get involved in the fun.

Distractions also limit the capacity of your puppy to relieve himself. If you take him out to relieve himself and he is distracted, he might not actually do it, he will most likely go back in the house and relieve himself.

## Feed him well

A dog could bark and whine as a result of experiencing hunger. You do not have to wait until he starts complaining about food.

Create a feeding schedule. Dogs love schedules. And ensure that he gets fed when the time is due. The right combination of food, toys, and sleep will elevate your canine friend to untold levels of ecstasy.

## Socialize him

Dog owners seem to think that socializing a dog involves taking him to a daycare. That is a great method of socializing, but it is quite expensive.

How about letting him play with other pets and kids? This will make him less aggressive and more welcoming to people, and critters. His instinctual barks will decrease and possibly even disappear altogether.

## Medical checkups

Most dog owners wait until it is obvious that their puppy is in need of medical attention. When you are attentive, the early signs are enough to spur you into action.

Taking a puppy for a medical checkup will ensure that you keep the illnesses at bay. When your puppy is healthy, it will be unlikely he will cry and complain.

# Chapter 12: Crate Training Your Dog for Travel

If you are traveling and you intend to bring your puppy along, ensure that he is contained in an appropriate crate, in case he gives you a rough time. If you are traveling by air, your crate must be IATA-compliant.

If you are driving, always confine your puppy for his safety. A crate allows the puppy to have his own space in which he can feel safe.

When he is taken out to a new location, he is unlikely to get scared. Crate training your puppy is really important when traveling, as it lets your puppy have their own space and allows you to set boundaries.

## Prepare early enough

You should start preparing as soon as you know that you are traveling. Buy the right size and do your research when purchasing a dog crate.

Ensure that you have taken the measurements of your dog. The crate must be big enough to allow him to stand, sit down and turn around comfortably.

The crate should be made of heavy-duty plastic with a metal grill door. Latches, clips, and dials should be made of sturdy material.

The crate should also be properly ventilated and has bedding. When you start crate training your puppy early enough, he will get used to his new space, and will not give you trouble during the travel.

## Normalize the travel crate

Encourage your puppy to get inside by putting treats and toys in the crate. Start feeding your puppy inside the crate so that he can get used to it.

When he gets familiar with the crate, he will start going in and out on his own will and even develop an attachment to his personal space.

Start closing the door for a short period of time and then gradually extend the time, and then put the crate in the car and drive over short distances so that he may feel what it is like to be driven around.

Here are some of the reasons why it is crucial to crate train your dog while preparing for a journey.

- **Makes traveling easier**

  Traveling with your dog unrestrained can be very hectic and dangerous. Puppies have high energy. They will keep moving around, and you will have to constantly watch them in case they hurt themselves. If you are traveling by air, it beats logic not to confine your canine friend.

- **Good behavior**

  A crate trained dog is responsive to commands than an untrained dog. A crate trained dog will exhibit the best manners during the journey and will not be difficult to control.

On the other hand, an untrained dog would be difficult to handle and is likely to behave in a manner that you disapprove of. For instance, you might call him, and he refuses to come.

- **Reduces damage**
  When you confine your canine friend, you restrict him from engaging in various activities which can cause damage. Chewing is one of the pastimes of puppies that usually results in damage.

  Your puppy has no regard to your valuable items so he will gnaw even at costly items like shoes and furniture.

- **Safety**
  If you are traveling by car, he is safe in his private space. If you are traveling by air, confining your canine friend would keep him safe, considering that it is easy to lose him to the crowd.

- **Helps him settle in a new location**
  When you move to a new location, it will be easier for your puppy to adjust because he still has his private space.

- **Allows you to enjoy your journey**

  Driving while watching your puppy at the same time, can be dangerous and can ruin the experience. If you confine him to his crate, it relieves you of the worry, and you can enjoy your journey.

- **Bad weather**

  Puppies are scared of going out when the weather is bad. It scares them so much that they sometimes become unable to relieve themselves. However, when they are confined to their crates, they tend to get over their anxiety quicker.

## Chapter 13: How Long Does it Take to Crate Train Your Puppy?

Getting a new dog has its challenges. The dog has to adapt to a new environment and has to deal with being separated from his former family.

As the dog owner, you may want to spend the whole day with your dog, but it is unrealistic because you need to go to work. Considering that your puppy is going to stay in the house for a long period of time while you are away, it is practical to confine him in a crate.

Crating your puppy is not meant to be a form of cruelty, but some dog owners make the mistake of letting the puppies stay in their crates for a long period of time. When a puppy is held in a crate for a prolonged amount of time, he is likely to develop anxiety and depression, and he will become vulnerable to certain illnesses due to the lack of exercise.

## Crate training during the day

Puppies are active during the day. The appropriate amount of time that you can leave your puppy inside the crate is informed by his age and his ability to control both his bladder and bowel movement.

According to the ASPCA, a puppy that is no more than eight weeks old should not be held in a crate for longer than an hour. When he crosses the eight-week old threshold, you may gradually increase the amount of time that you confine him in the crate.

From 14 to 16 weeks old, you can hold him in the crate for three to four hours. For puppies that are 17 weeks old and beyond, you should not confine them for more than six hours. Regardless of his age, you should never hold him in his crate longer than he can control his bladder and bowel movement.

## Crate training at night

If your puppy has developed an attachment to his crate as most puppies do, he will love nothing more than retiring to his "den" after jumping around throughout the day. At night he will be asleep and obviously much less active than during the day, but still, you have to awaken to take him out if he cannot control his bladder or bowel movement throughout the night.

## Crate training while you are at work

Most people crate train their puppies simply because they cannot afford to be around the whole day to watch him. A crate allows them to keep their puppy safe while they go to work.

A puppy must not be left in the crate for more than five hours. If you work near your home, you have to come back at appointed times to take him out.

If that is not possible, then consider enlisting the services of another person to help you. Keeping your puppy in the crate for a prolonged time can trigger depression and anxiety. If you cannot find another person to take him out, you need to construct a playing section within the house where your puppy can have free reign throughout the day.

# Chapter 14: When Should You Stop Crate training Your Puppy?

A crate provides security and shelter for your puppy, and it also allows the owner to be at peace. Dog trainers' advocate for all dogs to be crate trained.

Crating saves the dog owner a lot of trouble, especially when it comes to the chewing habit of most puppies. Puppies tend to chew at things, even though they could be expensive things like shoes and expensive mats.

There also comes a time where you have to stop crating the dog. It all depends on the dog in question and the circumstances of the dog owner.

## His personality

Assume that you have two dogs of different breeds. One of the dogs tends to lie down and stay in one place for an extended amount of time, while the other dog loves to jump around and chew up things.

In this case, it is alright to stop crating the first dog, but you should continue crating the second dog, in case he ruins valuable items. When your dog consistently demonstrates that he is up to no harm, then he can be trusted to be by himself.

However, if your dog has high-energy and adrenaline, the worst mistake you can do is leave him by himself while you are away.

## Extreme separation anxiety

If your dog has proven incapable of handling being alone, you might as well consider putting him off the crate. This will make him at peace.

When a dog is first put in the crate, the obvious reaction is rebellion. He ends up rebelling against his new home for a certain period of time, then he adapts to his new environment.

Sadly, some dogs never seem to adjust to living in the crate. It is actually a form of torture when you leave them there under the assumption that they will eventually come into terms with it.

When you find out that your dog cannot handle the anxiety that comes with being separated from you, you might want to look for an alternative to crating. When you are absent, he may exhibit behaviors like whining and barking endlessly.

## He is housetrained

A housetrained dog will exhibit appropriate potty manners. He will resist defecating indoors as he is aware that it annoys you. It would be okay to stop crating such a dog.

When he knows all that is expected of him, you will not have to run around after him to ensure that he does not stray. A housetrained dog exhibits pleasant manners. He understands the various actions by him that would upset you and tries not to do them.

## Does not chew

The problem of chewing items is much more pronounced in puppies than older dogs. Puppies are going through the initial stages of teething.

Puppies explore their surrounding using their mouth, and they find chewing things almost irresistible. If you are not careful, your puppy could chew expensive things and set you many thousands back.

It is also a dangerous habit, considering that the material he chews might affect his digestive system and give rise to all sorts of complications. This habit of chewing things persists even beyond the initial stages of a dog.

When you guide your dog into understanding that chewing things is not okay, he would eventually drop the habit. If your dog has gotten rid of the habit, it is okay not to crate him.

You can let him roam around the house, knowing too well that he will not be tempted to chewing your things again.

## Bad weather

If you live in an area with hostile climatic conditions, you should discontinue crating your dog. For instance, if your region suddenly becomes hot, it would be cruel to still keep your dog in his crate, as his temperature would rise and the limited ventilation of the crate will not help matters.

Similarly, if your area of residence suddenly grew cold, you should keep him out of the crate as the cold would get to him. During stormy seasons, your dog gets too scared, and you might want to reassure him by having him stay close to you.

## Medication

When you take your dog to the vet office, he might receive treatment that will make him very vulnerable. The doctor might advise against putting him in the crate until he gets well.

# Chapter 15: Common Problems You Might Run Into

Crate training your dog is not a walk in the park. It takes patience and persistence to achieve the results that you desire. In the end, it pays off as you have a well-behaved dog. Here are some of the challenges you might run into while crate training:

## Chewing

Puppies are particularly guilty of this habit. Since they explore the world around them using their small mouths, puppies often chew up things.

He might go around searching for things to chew as a way of calming himself. This is a major challenge because he will often chew at valuable things.

If you contain him in a plastic crate, he might also start chewing the plastic material in an attempt to break free from the confinement. This habit of chewing things does not just make you lose things, but also it poses serious health concerns to the puppy.

The material that he chews could affect the normal function of his intestines. You do not have to fight away this habit, but rather offer him guidance on the chewable and non-chewable things.

You can achieve this by introducing chewable toys. This will allow him to indulge his natural instinct of gnawing at things, albeit in a safe and fun way. If you catch him chewing things that he should not, just warn him sternly against repeating the mistake.

## Not coming when you call him

It can get frustrating when your dog fails to heed your calls. Whenever you call to him, and he ignores you, never assume that he has acquired a snobbish attitude without first establishing what is causing him to ignore you.

Also, do not get mad at him or even worse, do not hurt him. Always praise your dog whenever he comes to you.

This will make him associate the action of coming to you with getting praised. If your dog is still unresponsive to your calling him, do not run after him. Instead, take backward steps as you call on him and if it still does not work, order him to sit and go get him.

## Separation anxiety

Dogs quickly establish bonds with their owners. Some dogs are good at withstanding being alone while others are not so good.

Puppies are particularly needy. Separation anxiety in a puppy is triggered the moment he sees that you are about to leave him, which scares him.

Reassure your puppy that everything is alright, and you will be back soon. Get him a chewable toy that he can play with while you are not around. Make sure that you do not make a big deal of leaving or coming back home, as it will intensify his feelings of attachment.

## Whining

Puppies love expressing their needs through whining. It can be especially exhausting when your puppy will not keep quiet, especially at the night.

There are various reasons why a puppy whines, it could be a medical issue, getting scared, separation anxiety, hunger, boredom, or as a way of seeking attention. When your puppy whines do not yell at him, as it could scare him and make him withdraw.

Try to establish what is troubling your puppy and if you cannot come around it, then consider taking him to a vet for a checkup.

## Barking at the door

On the occasion that your puppy is pumped enough, he might graduate from mere whining and start barking. This is usually a way of getting your attention.

For instance, your puppy could be uncomfortable with being held in the crate, and he could bark incessantly as a way of expressing his rebelliousness. Ceaseless barking might also be indicative of an awaiting threat.

Try to establish whether there is a foreign object inside his crate that is scaring him. If the barking is so extreme that neighbors come to complain about it, you might want to take your puppy for a checkup and maybe put him on medication.

# Biting

Your dog could develop a tendency of biting – either people or critters. This indicates a level of distrust.

Focus on making him as comfortable as can be when he is around other people. You can achieve this by developing his social skills.

For instance, you may take him to a daycare and let him socialize with his kind. This will make him more welcoming to other people and other pets.

When your dog has a problem with biting, it could limit your social life, as some people might get scared of being near him.

# Accidents

In most cases, accidents are as a result of poor leadership on the part of the dog owner. But all in all, accidents are to be expected.

Do not hurt or yell at your dog, such reactions would scare him and make him scout for a more private area to relieve himself next time. Understand that puppies need to be shown the same thing over and over again.

With enough practice, his potty manners will eventually become fitting. Another major cause of accidents is medical problems.

If your puppy has diarrhea, he will not be able to control his bowel movement. If his urinary tract is infected, he will not be able to control his bladder.

Find out whether he is allergic to some of the foods that you are giving him, and if you cannot understand the triggers of the accident, it is time to take him to the vet for a checkup.

# Conclusion

Subtly introduce the crate to your puppy. For instance, you can put a treat in the crate and place the puppy near the entrance.

He is likely to scurry in and devour the treat. When he gets in do not be too quick to shut the door, but rather give him some time to explore the crate.

Dogs have a natural denning instinct, and they adore the solitude that crates give them. If he appears satisfied with the crate, you can shut the door and move away.

Gradually increase the amount of time that you leave him in the crate, but always ensure that you take him out so that he can relieve himself. When selecting the crate for your puppy, you have to ensure that it fits him perfectly.

He should be able to stand up, sit down, and turn around comfortably. If the crate is too big, he might convert one end of the crate into his potty and the other end as his sleeping quarters.

Always guide your puppy with patience and persistence until he acquires all the habits that you deem appropriate.

# Potty Training Your Puppy

## The Easiest Way to Teach Your Puppy Where And When to Go Potty

Kenneth Harrison

mentioned are done without written consent and can in no way be considered an endorsement from the trademark holder.

# Table Of Contents

# Introduction:

Puppies probably no scratch that puppies are the cutest thing on planet earth. They're cute, cuddly, and absolutely adorable!

The thing is though puppies don't know how to control their bowel movements. That's where we come in as pet owners.

It's up to us to help teach our puppies where and when to use the bathroom as we help them explore this new and exciting world. Potty training your puppy isn't the easiest thing that you'll ever do.

However, all you have to do is take one quick look at your adorable puppy and you'll be reminded that it'll all be worth it in the end. Thankfully though, this book will allow you to avoid many of those hardships that pet owners commonly have to go through.

You'll learn everything you need to know to potty train your puppy as soon as possible! The only thing left is to learn what you need to do and then actually do it. So let's jump in and get started!

# Chapter 1: Why What You Feed Them Matters

You might think it's odd that the first thing we're going to be talking about is dog nutrition. The thing is tough, what you feed your dog will greatly impact the potty training process.

If you're a bit skeptical right now, it's ok I understand, let me explain...

## The Difference Between High and Low-Quality Dog Food

Have you ever wondered why some dog food can cost upwards of $60-$70 per bag while others only cost $20-$30 for the same size bag? Isn't dog food dog food?

It's not like your puppy cares right? Well actually, what you feed your puppy does make a huge difference.

So why is it that some dog foods are way more expensive than others? What it comes down to are the ingredients that are used in the dog food.

Cheaper dog foods will use fillers in their dog foods. This will allow them to increase the poundage of the dog food as cheaply as possible.

More expensive dog foods will instead use high quality and natural ingredients to comprise all of their dog food.

Right now you might be thinking so what? I don't care if my dog food uses fillers.

My puppy still eats it and gets full so what does it matter? It matters a great deal because you have to stop and think why it is your puppy is eating in the first place.

Puppies don't eat food for the sake of eating food, there's a reason behind it. There are certain nutrients your puppy needs in order for his or her body to continue functioning.

Once those nutritional needs are met, then your puppy will be full. Therefore if you're feeding your dog a cheap food that contains less of the nutrients your puppy needs, your pup will have to eat more of it to get full.

Conversely, feeding your dog a high-quality food will allow your dog to get full eating less food. On the surface when you're at the pet store, it might appear as if it's cheaper to buy the less expensive food.

However, you're going to have to buy that food more often because your dog will need to eat more of it, so in the long run, it evens out. In addition to that, here's the big kicker—your puppy will have to use the bathroom more often if you feed him or her cheap dog food.

Think for a second about what poop and pee are—it's waste right? It's what your dog's body didn't use or absorb so the rest was excreted as waste.

If you're feeding your puppy a food that contains a bunch of fillers, do you think your puppy's body is going to be able to use those filters for anything? No of course not, it's junk!

Now your puppy is going to have to use the bathroom more often to excrete the fillers that are in the dog food you're feeding him or her. And of course the more often your dog has to use the bathroom, the harder it's going to be to train him or her.

## What Should You Look for in a Dog Food?

Hopefully, you now understand the importance of feeding your puppy a high-quality dog food. But now the question is, what should you feed your puppy?

The first thing you'll want to make sure of is that you feed your puppy a formula specifically made for puppies if he or she is less than a year old. The reason for this is because these formulas are higher in protein, which will help with your dog's growth and weight.

Puppies are active and they need the extra protein. As your dog gets older, you'll need to get an appropriate food for his or her current age.

After that, there are a couple of things you'll want to look out for. The first one is the price.

The old phrase, you get what you pay for is usually right and it certainly is in this case. So check the price and see if it's on the cheaper or higher end of dog foods.

If it's on the cheaper side, then your best bet is to avoid it simply because it'll likely be guilty of the things I'm about to discuss. Of course this isn't the case 100% of the time, so it doesn't hurt to double check. However, usually there's a reason why it's a cheap dog food.

After checking the price, the first thing you want to look at is the list of ingredients. The first ingredient listed on the label is what is contained the most in the dog food.

So for example, if the first ingredient on a label is chicken meal, then percentage wise chicken meal is the highest when compared to all of the other ingredients in the food.

That's important to understand because if the first two ingredients are low quality, then that means a large percentage of the dog food is low quality. So what should you be looking out for ingredient wise?

The first thing is the protein source. This is usually going to be the first ingredient listed on the label.

In most cases that's usually going to be something along the lines of beef, fish, or chicken. You want to look and see if the label says chicken meal for example.

The word "meal" is what you want to be on the lookout for. As an example, chicken meal is rendered chicken meat that includes flesh, skin, and/or accompanying bone.

As you can see that's pretty vague and allows companies room to use a little amount of flesh or a lot of flesh could be used. It can be hard to tell simply from the label so make sure you do your research on a dog food company before buying.

Meal byproduct isn't necessarily a bad thing—a lot of dog food companies use it. You just want to make sure if your dog food does use chicken meal for example that you look into it because not all meal byproduct is the same!

Preferably, you would get a dog food that contains something like deboned chicken or a deboned protein source. This is a clean source of skin and flesh.

You know you're getting the real deal if a deboned protein source is listed on the ingredient label. After the protein source, you'll want to look at the next listed ingredient.

In cheaper dog foods this is usually going to be something along the lines of corn or soybean meal. Corn especially is a low-quality filler ingredient that dogs have trouble digesting.

Many dogs also have allergies to certain ingredients like corn and this can cause them to scratch. On higher quality dog foods, you'll usually see something along the lines of brown rice, whole ground barley, or oatmeal.

These, of course, aren't the only high-quality ingredients, but they're some you need to be on the lookout for. At the end of the day, the best thing you can do is research and get expert advice on what food would be best to fit your puppy's specific needs!

## How Often Should You Feed Your Puppy?

Another thing you need to consider as a pet owner is how often you want to feed your puppy. Pet owners commonly make the mistake of free feeding their puppy.

Free feeding is where you leave food in your dog's bowl at all times and your puppy can eat whenever he or she pleases. There's a big problem with this.

If your puppy eats at random times, then that means he or she will poop at random times too! Therefore if you control when your puppy eats, you'll also be able to control when your puppy poops as well.

This will make potty training much easier! Puppies are young, active, and growing, therefore you'll need to feed your puppy often, which will usually be around 3-4 times per day depending on your schedule.

You'll simply feed your puppy and then take away the food after 15 minutes. If you're gone at work, simply feed your puppy before leaving, come back during lunch if possible, and then feed again sometime after work.

As you're going to find out, the key with potty training comes down to control. And it starts with what and how you feed your dog.

Following this advice will make things much easier for you! Finally, you might be wondering about water.

Should you restrict your puppy's water access like you would with food? The answer to this is no!

You definitely want to make sure your puppy has access to clean water throughout the day. The last thing you want to worry about is if your puppy is dehydrated or not.

Again remember that puppies are active and they'll need lots of water especially if they're playing outside in the heat. Your puppy might even be having so much fun that he or she forgets how thirsty he or she is!

Therefore, make sure that you give your dog access to water throughout the day. The only thing you might want to consider doing is taking away the water bowl 2 hours before bedtime.

This way you won't have to worry about your pup having an accident during the middle of the night.

# Chapter 2: How to Control Your Puppy's Environment for Success

When it comes to potty training your puppy, controlling the environment that your dog is in is the real key to success. And as the pet owner, it's your job to ensure that you do a good job of putting your puppy in an environment where it can succeed.

The better job you do of controlling where your dog goes, the better you'll be able to potty train your dog. This, of course, can be very difficult in the beginning.

Always keeping an eye on where your pup is at can certainly be tedious and a lot to keep up with. However, don't worry I'll share with you some tips on how to make this easier later on in this chapter.

For now, let's get into the basics of how dogs like to go about doing their business:

## Where Do Dogs Like to Do Their Business?

The first thing you need to know is that dogs don't like to go to the bathroom where they live and sleep. For example, if you had an outside dog with a doghouse in the backyard, it's very unlikely that your dog will use the bathroom inside of his or her doghouse.

The doghouse is his or her spot. It's his or her living area where he or she sleeps.

It's also a very small and confined area, thus making it even easier for your dog to know that this is her or her territory. Your dog isn't going to go inside the doghouse when he or she can simply go outside of the doghouse and use the bathroom anywhere outside.

However, things are much different when you take things inside and have a house dog. Now things are more confusing to the dog.

Your puppy doesn't understand that the entire house is his or her territory, and that going outside is the place to use the bathroom. Instead, your dog might think your bedroom is his or her territory and the rest of the house is his or her playground to do whatever he or she wants including using the bathroom.

And unfortunately, some pet owners get mad when their puppy uses the bathroom inside. This isn't the dog's fault, he or she is only using the bathroom outside of the vicinity of what he or she thinks is his or her primary residence.

In fact, getting mad at your dog will only make the problem worse. Your dog won't understand why he or she is getting into trouble.

Now your puppy will think it's bad to use the bathroom in front of you, so it'll start being more secretive about where and when he or she uses the bathroom. This is why controlling the area or space that your puppy has access to in the beginning is key.

## How to Control Your Puppy's Space for Potty Training Success

Successfully potty training your pup comes down to one thing— getting your puppy to use the bathroom where you want him or her to go. That's really all it is.

You can break that down one more step and say that you need your dog to avoid going potty in one area first and then go potty in another area. This section is going to focus more on how to get your puppy to not go potty in certain areas (i.e. your house).

As I talked about in the previous section, controlling where your dog goes in your house is important because your puppy won't use the bathroom in areas that he or she believes to be his or her space. This is why initially you must limit the space that your dog has access to.

You must first and foremost get your puppy accumulated to one room in your house before moving on and trying to get your dog accumulated to the rest of the house. And this is where the hard part comes in.

Keeping your dog in one room or area of your house all of the time is a hard thing to do. However, the better you are at controlling this, the better things will be for potty training. The laxer you are with this, the longer and harder it's going to be to potty train your pup.

Therefore the first thing you need to do is make things easy on yourself. If you don't have any tools to help you out here, it's going to be very difficult to keep your puppy in a confined space.

Your puppy will try to run all over the house, and you'll have no way of keeping him or her in a certain area. Imagine if you were working to fix a sink without any tools!

That's what it would be like to keep your puppy in a confined area without any supplies—it simply won't happen. You must consider what you're going to want to use to control your puppy's environment.

The first option you have is to use a puppy playpen. Most playpens are a good size so your puppy will have some room to run around and play in.

You'll also have space for a food and water bowl, blankets, toys, and a pet bed. It's also convenient too because when you want to play or interact with your puppy, you can take him or her out of the pen, and then put him or her back in the pen once play time is over.

Over time you can start to move the pen to different areas of the house so your dog will learn that more and more of the house is his or her territory. Secondly, you can use a dog leash.

You'll attach the leash to your belt buckle using a clip and then attach the other end to your puppy's collar. This way your puppy can't get too far away from you, and you'll be able to control exactly where it is your dog does and doesn't go.

One problem with this, however, is the fact that your puppy won't be able to go with you everywhere around the house. You must accumulate your puppy to one room of the house at a time.

So if you're going to be in one room for a long period of time, then this is a great option you can use during those times, or in general when you feel like changing things up from using a playpen or something.

On the other hand, if you're going to be around the house a lot to do chores, this isn't going to be a good option. It's key to make sure your puppy stays within a confined space before you expand his or her horizons.

Sticking with the leash option you could also attach the leash to a sturdy object. This isn't better than something like a playpen because it gives your puppy a lot less freedom to be able to move around and play.

However, if you find yourself in a pinch, you can use this as a way to make sure your dog will stay in the area he or she needs too. Of course ideally, you'll be able to interact with and keep an eye on your dog for a good period of the day, which would limit the amount of time your dog would need to be in a playpen or on a leash in the first place.

Another thing you can use is pet gates. This is a solid option because you can block off entrances to other parts of the house and give your puppy more freedom to be able to move around and play.

You'll be able to confine your pup to whatever part of the house you need to. This might not always work though as you try to expand your dog's territory. For example, in my house, the entrance to the kitchen is very wide and open.

There's not a pet gate long enough to cover the entrance, so I'd have to use something else to keep my puppy in the living room and out of the kitchen. Aside from that, however, this option is quite the ideal choice.

Finally, you have the pet crate. This can work as an option if you're trying to potty train your dog while you're gone at work.

In general though, when you're at the house, this isn't going to be a good option. You don't want to have your puppy locked up in a crate for long periods of time while you're at home.

Your puppy isn't going to have any room to move or play. So it's best to avoid using this when you're at home potty training your dog.

## How Long Should You Wait to Expand Your Puppy's Territory?

You're probably wondering how long you should wait before moving your dog into other areas of the house and expanding his or her territory. There's no one-way to go about it.

However, with that being said, you want to make sure that your dog fully knows the current room he or she is in is his or her territory before moving onto another room. It would be a mistake to move your puppy to the kitchen when your puppy had an accident in the living room the day before.

That's why a good rule of thumb is to play it safe when it comes to expanding your puppy's territory. If you're unsure that your dog isn't fully trained in one area of your house, then wait until you are sure before moving onwards.

So for example, if your dog goes two weeks without having an accident in a certain room, then you could go ahead and move to the next room. Of course, you can move onto another area sooner than that if you feel confident your dog is ready to, but don't feel like you have to rush into things. Take your time with it and make sure you're going at a pace your puppy can handle!

## Logistics of Expanding Your Dog's Territory

The last thing you'll want to consider is the logistics of how you'll expand your dog's territory. For example, it wouldn't make much sense to house train your dog in the kitchen and then move the dog to your bedroom if the living room is in between those two rooms.

You want to progress with this using adjacent rooms. So for example, if you start to house train your puppy in the kitchen, then the next room you expand to should be the room right next to the kitchen.

So if that room is the living room for example, then that's the next room you're going to train your dog in. Now once your dog is trained in one room, for example, they can go in that room.

You don't want to completely isolate your puppy to one room at a time or else he or she might forget that the old room is his or her territory and instead think only the new room is his or her territory.

Therefore the best thing you can do once you start expanding into new areas of your house is to heavily supervise your dog at times where he or she is allowed to go into all areas he or she has been trained in.

So for example, if you're expanding your puppy's territory from just the kitchen to the living room and kitchen, you want to give your puppy some time to roam around both rooms.

Again this time needs to be heavily supervised because your dog doesn't fully understand the living room is his or her territory yet. Your puppy might run into the living room and go poop.

So by giving your dog access to both rooms at certain times, you'll be able to ensure you're puppy is able to make a smooth transition without forgetting that the old room is still his or her territory.

This isn't going to be something you'll be able to do all of the time of course. It's more of something you'll do from time to time when you have the chance to heavily supervise and play with your puppy.

Normally your puppy will be in his or her playpen in a single room that you're currently training him or her in if that's the method you're using.

From time to time though, when you take your puppy out to play, make sure you let him or her go to old areas of the house that you've trained him or her in.

If you're using the pet gate method, don't give your dog access to both the new and old rooms while you're gone at work. Let's say you trained your dog in the kitchen and then expanded your dog's area to the living room.

Don't use the gate to block off rooms to where your puppy can go to both the living room and the kitchen. Block rooms off to where your puppy will only be in the living room or the new room you're currently training your puppy in.

The reason for this is because once you leave to go to work, your puppy will go poop or pee in the new room because he or she thinks the kitchen is his or her territory and not the living room.

Therefore by isolating your puppy to the new room (the living room in this case) while your gone, your puppy will realize that this room is part of his or her new territory too.

Then when you come home, if you have an hour or two to supervise your puppy, you can allow access to both rooms. However, the majority of the time your puppy will be isolated to the current room that you're training him or her in.

# Chapter 3: How to Potty Train Your Puppy While You're at Work

You might be thinking that all of this information sounds good so far, but how do you potty train your puppy if you're at work for 8 hours a day? What if you're not able to constantly control your dog's environment?

These are great questions to consider because most people aren't going to be at their house all of the time. So what should you do in these cases?

The first thing you'll want to do is set up the right environment for your puppy while you're gone. This is critical.

The reason for this is because puppies can only hold their bladder for up to one hour for each month old that they are. For example, a 12-week old puppy can only hold his bladder for up to 3 hours.

And if you're gone for 8 or more hours, then there's likely going to be a "surprise" waiting to be cleaned up when you get home. Here are some options you can consider if you're going to be gone from your home for hours at a time:

## Using a Crate

One option that you have is to use a crate. This is a good option because you won't have to worry about your puppy causing any trouble while you're gone, and it can be a good way to control their environment while you're potty training.

One downside, however, is that your dog won't be able to use the potty in the crate. You don't want the dog to associate using the bathroom with its crate.

You want the dog to associate his crate like a child would with his bedroom. You want it to be a fun and relaxing place, not a place where he or she uses the bathroom.

That's why it's important to get the right sized crate. You want the crate to be just big enough for your pup to be able to lay down, sit up, and turn around once.

If the crate is any bigger than this than your dog will be able to use the bathroom on one side of the crate and sleep on the other. If you want to buy a bigger crate for your dog to be able to grow into, that's perfectly fine, just make sure that you get a divider so you can section off a portion of the crate and make it the correct size for your puppy's current size.

Therefore, if your dog can't go to the bathroom in the crate, and it can only hold it's bladder for so long, then you're going to need to come home on your lunch break to take it outside. Not only will this give your puppy the chance to go potty, but your dog will also get to exercise.

Exercise is key for puppies because they have a lot of energy, and it's necessary for proper growth. This'll give your puppy a little break and allow them to move more freely than they could while locked in a crate.

If it's not practical for you to come home on your lunch break, then you'll need to get a friend, family member, or dog sitter to come and let your puppy out. This really is the key to successfully training your dog in a crate.

The idea of leaving your dog in a crate for 8 hours a day sounds easy, but it's going to be hard for the dog not to use the bathroom. Therefore, if you're not able to come home during a break at work or get someone else to let your dog out, it's best to consider a different option.

## Set Up a Potty Safe Room in the House

If you're unable to come home during work, then a better option may be to set up a potty safe room in your house that your puppy will stay in while you're gone. Now, this room isn't potty safe because it's okay for your dog to use the bathroom in this room, it's a potty safe room because if an accident does happen, it'll be easy to clean up.

That's why you'll want to set up this area in a room of your house such as the laundry room where there are linoleum or tile floors. That way if an accident does occur, it'll be much easier to clean up than if the accident happened on the carpet.

To set up this room, you'll want to use a pet gate to block off access to the rest of your house. Depending on your house set up, you could also close the door to your potty safe room.

However, I would recommend against this as it might make your dog feel more like it's locked up in prison and being punished. With the pet gate, your puppy will at least be able to look out and see more of its surrounding environment.

Aside from that, you'll also want to make sure that you put a food and water dish inside the room as well. It's important for your puppy to stay hydrated and well fed while you're gone for long periods of time.

Now free feeding your dog isn't something that I usually recommend as you learned in the last chapter. However, you might have a long commute or be unable to come home to feed your dog during your lunch break.

If this is the case, then it may be best to leave a food bowl in your puppy's safe room or playpen. It's not ideal, but it'll work if you find yourself in a tough situation.

The key to this is to get the correct feeding and drinking bowls. Puppies can be clumsy, so you'll want to avoid getting a glass or ceramic bowl that can possibly break.

The shattered pieces could get in your puppy's paws or your puppy may accidentally try to eat part of the bowl while you're gone. That's why the best kind of water bowl you can get is a non-spill water bowl.

This way you can ensure that your puppy will have a constant source of water while you're gone. On the other hand, if your dog knocks over its water bowl, then it won't have anything to drink for the rest of the day until you get back.

As for a food bowl, getting a non-spill bowl isn't as important because your dog can still eat off the ground if it wants to. Of course, you'll still have to clean up a mess, but it's not critical like it is with the water bowl.

Simply getting a stainless steel or plastic food dish will suffice. Aside from that, you'll also want to include some toys to keep your pup entertained and a pet bed for napping and sleeping.

The final thing you'll need to get is puppy pads. This'll allow your puppy to be able to use the bathroom while you're gone. So be sure to check out the later section in this chapter for how to train your dog using potty pads!

## Use a Puppy Play Pen

The other option you have is to use a puppy playpen. These pens come in different heights and sizes, so be sure to get one that's appropriate for your dog's current size.

The cool thing is that most puppy playpens are adjustable, which allows you to manipulate the size and shape to better fit your house. One positive to using the puppy playpens is that you'll be able to better control your puppy's environment to a confined area.

This'll help him or her establish a smaller area as his living space rather than the entire house, which can be troublesome. You'll also be able to choose where you want to put the playpen.

I'd recommend placing it somewhere where you want your puppy to spend the majority of its time initially even when you're home. This is to help better control the dog's environment and get it used to a certain area.

As for what you'll want to put in the playpen, the same things apply as with the potty safe room. You'll want a food and water dish (preferably stainless steel or plastic), toys, a pet bed, and a potty pad.

Nothing too fancy, just the basics to get the job done. Also depending on how cramped your laundry room is, this option will also give your dog more room to move around during the day, which is very important for puppies.

This is something, unfortunately, the puppy won't be able to do if it's in a crate, so I'd highly recommend that you do this or the puppy safe room if possible!

## Pros and Cons to Using Potty Pads

The one thing you will have to train your puppy to be able to do with the latter options is to be able to use a potty pad. There are pros and cons to using potty pads.

The first major benefit is that you don't have to worry about taking your dog outside all of the time. If you're gone for long periods of time, then your puppy will still be able to go potty if he or she needs to.

One con, however, is that using potty pads can make the transition to going outside a little bit harder. The reason for this is because is because dogs get used to going on the same type of surface whether that's concrete, grass, gravel, or cloth like in the case of most potty pads.

This might not seem like a big deal, but most dogs won't be able to tell the difference between the surface of a potty pad and something like a rug or carpet.

This can cause issues because if you decide to stop using potty pads, then your dog may still occasionally go on a rug or carpet because that texture feels the same to him or her and it's what your dog is used to.

One solution to this would be to get a turf or grass potty pad. This will better mimic the outside environment that you'll likely want your puppy to get used to going on.

Most of the grass potty pads are washable and porous, which will make the pee sink to the bottom rather quickly to a holding tray underneath. If you don't want to constantly have to clean the bottom tray, you can even place a disposable potty pad in between the turf and the bottom layer.

Of course, you don't have to get this type of a potty pad, but it will make things much easier for your dog to be able to associate where it needs to go to use the bathroom.

## How to Train Your Dog to Use the Potty Pads

Ok, so how do you actually go about getting your dog to use the potty pads? The first thing you'll need to do is set aside some time for you to actually train your dog to use the pads.

Simply placing a potty pad in a pen, going to work, and hoping for the best isn't going to cut it. You first need to look for signs that your dog needs to go to the bathroom.

Common signs a puppy might give are circling around the same area, sniffing, or restlessness. You'll grow more accustomed to your puppy's signs because he or she will generally do the same thing before going to the bathroom.

So be patient and look for patterns. Whenever you do notice that your dog needs to go to the bathroom, take your dog over to the potty pad.

Most pads are sprayed with an attractive scent that will encourage dogs to want to use them. Hopefully, when you bring your dog over to the pad, it'll go on the pad.

Once your puppy has finished its business on the pad, you'll want to immediately reward the behavior. Praise your dog and give him or her a treat.

Your dog will start to associate going on a potty pad with getting a treat, which will encourage that behavior in the future. You'll want to repeat this process as often as possible until your puppy really gets the hang of it.

This all comes down to controlling your puppy's environment and making sure that you keep an active eye on your dog. If you get any hint that your puppy needs to use the bathroom, immediately take him or her over to the pad.

Of course, your puppy likely isn't going to be perfect with this. Accidents will occur more than likely. If an accident does happen, be patient and act like nothing happened.

Don't scold your dog, simply clean up the mess and move on. I'll explain more on why this is in a later chapter, just avoid doing it for now.

Finally one last option you do have if you don't have time to potty pad train your dog is to put down multiple disposable potty pads in your pen or potty safe room. This way you'll increase the likelihood of your dog actually going on the pad.

The downside to this of course is that you'll have to use more pads, and if you don't use a pad holder or secure the pads to the ground, then your puppy will likely move them around and end up going on the floor instead of using the pad like he or she is supposed to.

# Chapter 4: Using a Bell to Train Your Puppy

One way that you can train your dog to use the bathroom outside is to train him or her to ring a bell by your door. This is a great idea to consider teaching your dog because it can sometimes be hard to tell when your dog needs to go out.

This can especially be true in the beginning when you don't know what your dog's signs are that he or she needs to use the bathroom. My Yorkie, Rocky, will bark when he wants to be let outside.

It can be a little annoying at times, but he gets his point across, and I can hear him wherever I'm at in the house. My other dog, Jake the beagle, will stand by the door and wait.

It's nice that's he's patient and doesn't bark, but sometimes he has to wait for a bit if I'm not in the area to see him at the door. Therefore by training your dog to ring a bell to go outside, you won't have to worry about your dog waiting for too long or have to deal with barking that can be annoying at times.

Of course, this isn't something you have to do, but it's nice to know how to go about doing it in case you are interested.

## What Type of Bell Should You Get?

The first thing you'll need to consider is what type of bell you want to get for your door. There are two main types you'll have to decide between.

The first one is a long strap that has multiple bells hanging off of it. You hang the strap around your doorknob.

The other kind is one that you would attach to your wall beside your door. The bell hangs out and away from a piece of metal so you don't have to worry about your dog scratching up your wall. Either option will work.

Another thing you might want to consider doing is getting two bells. You'd place one bell inside your house and the other one outside.

This way your dog will be able to ring the bell whenever he or she wants to be let back inside.

## Training Your Dog to Use a Bell

Once you have a bell the first thing that you want to do is get your dog used to the new object. Get your puppy familiarized with the bell.

So get comfortable and play with your dog, and then introduce the bell. Bring the bell around your dog.

You don't have to shove it in his or her face—just make sure he or she is aware of the bell. Let your puppy sniff it, look at it, or whatever else.

When your dog reacts favorably towards the bell, reward him or her with a treat. We want your puppy to start to associate good things with this new object.

The next step once your dog is comfortable with the bell is to go ahead and ring it a little bit. You don't need to go crazy with it and freak your dog out, but let him or her know that this new thing makes a sound.

Once again, if your dog reacts favorably (and by favorably that could be something as simple as your dog being neutral and not flipping out), then be sure to reward your pup with a treat.

Next, it's time to either hang the bell on your doorknob or on your wall. Now we're going to get your dog to interact with the bell. There's something you need to consider first though, and that is how you want your puppy to ring the bell.

115

Your dog can either brush his or her nose up against the bell or swipe at it with his or her paw. Either way will work, however, it might be more practical for your dog to use his or her nose so that you won't have to worry about any scratches on your door over time.

You'll want to do whatever you can to get your puppy to interact with the bell. So hold a treat close to the bell, and even if your pup accidentally nudges the bell then great—reward him or her with a treat.

You want to continue doing this cycle of your dog ringing the bell and getting rewarded until you feel like your puppy has a good handle of it. Even if you have to keep on getting your dog to inadvertently hit the bell, that's ok.

Eventually, your dog will start to pick up on the fact that ringing the bell is a good thing because he or she gets a treat when the bell is rung. Also don't be afraid to capitalize on the momentum.

If you've had a success with your dog ringing the bell, then don't be afraid to keep on going. If your dog keeps ringing the bell, then stop rewarding him or her—keep going and let your puppy really get the hang of things!

Stopping the rewards will only confuse your dog and make him or her wonder what actually needs to be done in order to get a treat. Consistency is the key here.

If you're worried about giving your dog too many treats to make this work, then break them up into tiny pieces. Or you could even consider a different type of reward.

You could give your dog praise, a belly scratch, or even through a ball to play fetch if your pup enjoys that. Once this step is complete, the next thing you want to do is start to transfer to your dog going outside.

Get him or her to ring the bell and then go outside with your dog. Once both you and your dog are outside, you can then reward your dog with a treat.

After a couple of times of doing this, all you need to do from this point is make your puppy ring the bell before he or she can go outside.

For example, if your dog is giving you some other sign that he or she needs to be let out, then go ahead and take your dog over to the door, but don't let him or her out until the bell is rung.

Eventually, your dog will start to pick up on the fact that when the bell is rung he or she gets to go outside. Be patient with this and give it some time, but soon enough your dog will consistently start to ring the bell when he or she wants to be let out.

Now the last thing you need to understand is that sometimes your puppy might ring the bell even if he or she doesn't need to use the bathroom. Your pup might ring the bell because he or she wants to go outside and not because he or she needs to use the bathroom.

It's okay if your dog does this, use your best judgment to determine if your dog needs to go or not. You don't have to let your puppy outside every time he or she rings the bell.

It's okay if you let your puppy out sometimes even if he or she doesn't need to use the bathroom. Don't worry too much about it, either way, just be happy your dog is trained to use a bell!

# Chapter 5: Common Pitfalls You'll Want to Avoid

When it comes to potty training your puppy there are quite a few mistakes that people regularly make. If you're able to avoid these pitfalls, you'll automatically give yourself a much higher chance of succeeding.

## Pitfall #1: Letting Your Guard Down Too Soon

This is something a lot of people fall for. They think that they can completely potty train their puppy over the course of a few days. Once those few days are up, they'll relax their training efforts.

When this happens, your puppy is more than likely going to slip up and have some accidents. This is because it can take months to fully potty train your puppy.

It really depends on the dog. Some dogs might pick things up rather quickly.

While for others, it could take them up to 6-8 months to fully get the hang of things. That's why it's so important for you to be patient and to have the right expectations heading into this journey.

It might be discouraging to think that it'll take months to get your dog fully potty trained, but think about it. If your puppy lives a long and full live (which hopefully it will), then even if it does take a full 6 months for your puppy to get the hang of things, then you'll still get to enjoy a long life of a well-trained dog.

So yes, you need to be patient and stay diligent in your efforts to potty train your dog. Keep up with it, and continue to use the tips and guidelines in this book.

Don't think that because your dog went a week without an accident that you're in the clear. Be sure that you keep a tight control on your puppy's environment and that you continue to reinforce positive behavior for months instead of days to make sure your puppy really has the hang of things.

## Pitfall #2: Punishing Your Puppy When Accidents Happen

There's not a perfect puppy that will go it's whole life without having an accident. Accidents will most certainly happen.

Therefore, the only variable in this equation is how you react to them. I understand that accidents can be quite frustrating, especially if they occur on the carpet.

This is something you're going to have to deal with throughout your dog's life—even if it's fully house trained. The reason why I say this is because I have two senior dogs.

One of them recently had the runs and there was a mess to clean up and be taken care of. It wasn't his fault of course, but it still happened.

I've also had to deal with throw up during their lives as well. The point is that owning a dog isn't always going to be perfect.

It's messy sometimes—heck, you could even say it's messy a lot in the beginning. But the positives of owning a dog and having a companion easily outweigh the negatives.

So why is it that you shouldn't punish your puppy when it has an accident indoors? The main reason is that if it already happened, then it's too late. Often times, people will see the pile of poop, then they'll take their puppy and stick his or her face in it and say, "bad puppy!"

The problem with this approach is that your dog doesn't exactly know what it is that he or she did wrong. The gap of time between when the accident happened to when you notice and try to correct the behavior is too long.

You want your dog to understand that it was wrong of him or her to use the bathroom inside, but at this point, your dog doesn't know that. You puppy needed to use the bathroom, so it did.

Then when your shove your puppy's face in the mess, he or she is going to think he's or she's getting into trouble for going poop in general. Your dog knows that it has to go to the bathroom, so he or she is going to be confused.

In the future, you'll likely notice that your puppy will be afraid to use the bathroom in front of you. That's because your puppy thinks it's doing something wrong.

So your puppy will start to go into a corner of the house and do his or her business there in an effort to hid it from you. And as you can probably guess, for most pet owners who don't know this is wrong, they'll only perpetuate the problem.

They'll then find the poop in the corner of a room and once again try to scold the behavior. The dog will then try to find new places to secretly go poop.

However, what should you do if you catch your puppy in the act? Let's say you notice your dog starting to squat like it's about to poop inside. What should you do?

Again, you don't want to punish the behavior. Instead, the first thing that you want to do is divert your dog's attention. So clap or make a loud noise.

You don't want the noise to be in a negative tone. You need to do something that will divert your puppy's attention from what it's trying to do.

Then immediately take your dog outside to the area where you want him or her to use the bathroom. If your dog goes outside like he's or she's supposed to, then be sure to immediately reward the behavior with a treat or something like that.

If you were a little too late and your puppy did most of its business inside (or on it's way outside), then that's ok. Don't reward the behavior unless your puppy went where you wanted him or her to.

In that case, simply clean up the mess and move on. Try to catch it earlier if you can.

Don't punish or reward the behavior because ultimately your puppy didn't use the bathroom outside. This is also another reason why spending more time and getting to know your puppy is critical.

You'll start to pick up on what your dog's behaviors are right before it needs to use the bathroom. You'll be able to act swiftly once you know these signs for your puppy.

Initially, though, you'll have no idea, so be patient in the beginning until you start to familiarize yourself with your dog's behaviors.

## Pitfall #3: Expecting Your Dog to Tell You When It Needs to Be Let Out

Another common mistake new dog owners make is that they expect their puppy to be able to tell them when it is that they need to go outside. Your puppy likely isn't going to give you any sort of sign that it needs to be let out.

As the pet owner, it's your responsibility to keep a watch on your puppy and look for signs that he or she needs to be let out. Of course, this isn't an easy thing to do.

Keeping a close watch and paying attention to signals over time certainly is easier said than done. That's why the best thing you can initially do is to take your dog out regularly.

Don't wait for a sign that your dog needs to go. Remember that puppies can only hold their bladder for up to 1 hour for each month old that they are.

So if you have a really young puppy, then your best bet is to take him or her out every 1-2 hours to be on the safe side. And when you do take your puppy out give him or her some time to actually use the bathroom.

Don't stay out there for 30 seconds and assume that your dog doesn't need to go. Stay outside for 5-10 minutes if you have to in order to make sure that your dog doesn't need to go.

Yes, this can be very tedious at times, but it's part of the process of raising a puppy, and it certainly beats having to clean up a mess in the house!

## Pitfall #4: Not Being Understanding of the Fact that Accidents Will Happen

One big pitfall people make is that they get frustrated when accidents happen. Yes, it is annoying to have to clean up a mess in your house, but again this comes with the territory of getting a new puppy!

Some people expect that their dog knows what he or she is doing is wrong when that simply isn't the case. Others think their dog will be perfect and never go inside, which is another incorrect line of thinking.

Unrealistic expectations like these only lead to more frustration in the end. Your puppy will never be good enough to fully meet what you expect out of him or her.

But think about it from the puppy's perspective. It's only a few weeks old, and he or she has the great big world to explore with all of these new and exciting things surrounding him or her.

Do you think that your dog is going to understand what a house is and that it's bad to go inside a house? A dog isn't born with instincts like that.

It must learn that it's bad to use the bathroom inside. And it's your job to be able to guide your dog and teach him or her well.

Learning how to go outside to use the bathroom is probably the last thing on your dog's mind! It's way more interested in chewing on things, playing, and napping!

Therefore, whenever accidents do happen, take a deep breath and understand that this is all part of the process. It'll be worth it in the end when you have a well-trained dog so stick with it!

Don't show any signs of negativity around your puppy. Your dog will be able to pick up on this and he or she might wonder what he or she did wrong.

The best thing you can do is not show any sort of reaction one way or the other, simply clean up the mess and move on.

## Pitfall #5: Not Rewarding Your Dog for Doing the Right Thing

This pitfall relates a lot to parenting. It can be easy to catch our kids in the act of doing something wrong and punish or correct the behavior.

But how often do kids get praised or reinforced when they do something good? A lot of times we're so focused on only correcting the bad behaviors that we forget to reward the good behaviors.

Think about this in your own life. When you're at work and you do a good job on a project how do you feel when your boss doesn't acknowledge you?

It doesn't feel good right! You probably don't need praise for everything you do, but it feels good to be recognized doesn't it?

On the flip side, compare that to when your boss does praise your good work and lets you know about it in some way. It makes you feel special and lets you know you're on the right track.

It also motivates you to work harder and to continue doing a good job. You're not even getting a raise or anything like that, you just want to continue working hard because you feel appreciated.

Your puppy is the same way. He or she needs to know that his or her behaviors are good and encouraged.

If you don't reward good behavior, then it'll be hard to build consistency with your puppy's behaviors. However, if you reward good behavior, then your dog will start to associate that behavior with a positive outcome.

And this doesn't have to be just rewarding your dog for using the bathroom. It can be for anything.

Maybe your dog stayed instead of jumping on someone or your dog didn't bark in a situation where he or she usually does.

These are behaviors that you need to reward with a treat, praise, or something like it. It'll help to encourage your dog to know that he or she is doing the right thing!

## Pitfall #6: Not Going Outside with Your Dog When He or She Needs to Go

It's easy to think that when your dog needs to go to the bathroom, you let him or her outside and that's it. However, there are a couple of problems in doing this.

The first one is that unless you're watching your dog from a window, you won't know if your dog actually went to the bathroom or not. You can't assume that because your dog went outside that he or she is going to know to use the bathroom.

There are plenty of things your dog will find outside to distract him or herself. Maybe your dog gets outside and then starts to chase a butterfly or squirrel.

Then your puppy forgets that he or she needed to use the bathroom until he or she comes in and goes potty inside. By staying outside with your dog, you'll ensure that your dog actually goes, and you'll be able to keep your puppy focused.

The other issue with not going outside with your dog is that you won't be able to reward the behavior. So even if your dog does use the bathroom outside, then your puppy won't know that was the right thing to do.

Your dog might continue to go outside or he or she might not. Essentially you're leaving it up to chance.

On the other hand, if you reward the behavior, then your puppy will know that what he or she did was a good thing. This'll be a much better way to ensure that your puppy will continue to use the bathroom outside.

# Chapter 6: The Potty Training Mindset You Need to Have as an Owner

A lot of times when it comes to doing and learning new things, we tend to focus on the mechanical aspect of the task. For example, when you're changing a tire, all you really need to know is how to change the tire.

You change it and move on that's it. However, when we're dealing with other people or animals, there's a big psychological component that's involved as well.

It's not as simple as saying do this and move on. There are a lot more emotions involved and each animal or person is unique and might respond differently depending on what the situation is.

So far, this book has focused on what you need to do and why you need to do it. However, I haven't talked much about the overall mindset you should approach these strategies with.

If I was simply teaching you how to change a tire for example, then this wouldn't be necessary because that task is primarily mechanical.

Unless of course, you were changing a tire on the side of the road in the dead heat of the summer, then maybe you'd need to apply some mindset techniques to get the job done, but I digress.

Regardless, here are some tips to help you approach potty training with the right attitude:

## Tip #1: Embrace the Hardships

There's no beating around the bush here—potty training your puppy is hard. It's not some one-time thing that you do and then forget about.

It requires constant care and dedication for weeks and months for your dog to fully get the hang of things. However, many dog owners want it to be easy.

They try to potty train their puppy over the weekend and think all is good. Then the dog will have an accident and they'll lose it.

You have to be patient from the get-go and understand there will be difficulties with lots of ups and downs. Ironically by embracing the hardships, it'll actually make thing easier as opposed to taking the path of least resistance.

And this holds true for many more areas of life than dog training. Imagine parenting for example.

When a child starts whining for a toy at the store, what do most parents do? They give in and get their kid the toy.

It's easier to get your kid the toy so he or she will stop throwing a fit rather than ignore them until they stop crying. However, doing so will only make your life harder.

Now that the kid whined and got his or her way, the child learned something—when I whine I get my way—I'm going to keep doing this!

Now every time the parent goes to the store the child will whine more and more, which means more toys will be bought, and in the end, things ended up being a lot harder than they should've been.

On the other hand, imagine the parent who does the hard thing and ignores or doesn't give into the behavior of the child. Eventually, the child will stop crying and begin to learn that crying doesn't work.

This, of course, will make your life easier because you'll soon enough be able to go to the store without your child even trying to cry. In much the same way, this is how you need to approach potty training your puppy.

If you embrace the hardships of strictly controlling your dog's environment and taking him or her outside regularly, then you'll make the process as smooth as possible.

However, if you get lazy and let your dog expand his or her territory to certain parts of the house too soon, or you forget to take your puppy outside, then it'll only take that much longer to potty train your pup.

This is the first and most important thing that you need to accept. You have to know what you're getting yourself into as a pet owner. Yes, there will be some difficult and tedious things you'll have to go through, but ultimately the pros outweigh the cons!

## Tip #2: Remember the Why

Sometimes when you're busy cleaning up your dog's accidents it can seem like it's not worth it. You have to be able to look past these shortcomings and see the bigger picture.

One way you can do this is by remembering your why. Think back and remember why you want to get a dog in the first place.

Maybe it was a rescue animal and you wanted to give him or her a good home and a better life. That's a very noble cause, so remember that when things aren't going the way you want them to.

Maybe think about where the animal would be today if you hadn't rescued him or her. Maybe you get lonely and you want a companion to be with you and comfort you.

That's another great reason to get a dog, so be sure to keep that on the front of your mind as well. Think about how comforting your dog is in difficult moments!

Or you possibly got a puppy because they're really cute and you couldn't resist. That's definitely a legitimate reason to get a dog!

In moments where the dog has accidents though, the puppy might not seem so cute. However, think about how innocent the puppy is and that it's not fully trained yet so he or she doesn't know better.

I mean it'll be hard to get mad at a sweet puppy-dog face! Ultimately though you do what you do as a pet owner out of love, and love requires sacrifices.

So be sure to always remember the why. Write it down with pen and paper and post it on your desk or someplace where you'll see it regularly. This is an easy way to ensure you always remember why it is that you're doing what you are for your dog!

# Tip #3: Have Patience

Patience is something that takes practice. It's easy to be patient in situations that don't require it.

It's hard to be patient during stressful moments like when you're stuck in traffic trying to get to work. However, it's during these tough moments where we can really learn and grow.

An example of this in my life was when I dog sat for my friend. He had just rescued this dog, and she was pretty wild to say the least!

She chewed on the blinds, chewed holes in my air mattress, had accidents in the apartment, and whined for hours when it was time for bed. It was quite a tough weekend for me especially because it wasn't my dog.

I was wondering what I had gotten myself into. This isn't my dog and I'm not the one responsible for training her I would tell myself!

But then I thought to myself, well he did rescue her. He's giving her a great home, and he really cares about doing the best he can to give her a good home and train her.

Sure he doesn't know everything about how to train dogs, but maybe I could help him out instead of complaining about it. Not only that, but he had just gotten the dog so of course she wasn't properly trained!

I had gotten a little too frustrated over my air mattress and that caused me to lose sight of what truly mattered. I learned that I had to be patient no matter what the situation was.

It didn't matter if it involved my dog or not. You might be at the dog park for example, and another dog might snap at yours.

Be patient in those moments. Try to help the situation however you can.

Or maybe someone else will be dog sitting for you. How would you want them to treat your dog?

The same way you would with love and care right? I get that it can be easy to simply say well just have patience!

But from now on, when you're in tough situations with your dog (or even someone else's dog for that matter) think about the bigger picture. You're in this for love and companionship so remember that.

If you're able to keep that at the front of your mind when things are hard, then I have no doubt that you'll be able to show patience. At the end of the day, that's what new puppies need is a lot of patience!

Giving your dog that deep love will only grow your bond deeper and stronger than ever!

## Tip #4: Set Goals

Another thing that can be helpful is to set potty training goals. These can help you to keep your focus and help you stay on track better when you're potty training your puppy.

The first thing you want to focus on is the outcome. Ask yourself what outcome is it you want to achieve by the end of this?

Most likely, it's going to be something along the lines of wanting to have a house trained dog that does his business outside and not inside. Then you want to write down that goal in the present tense as if it's already been achieved.

The reason for this is because your subconscious mind can't tell the difference between what you've actually achieved and what you haven't. Therefore by acting as if you've already achieved your goal, you can make your subconscious mind think that you've accomplished your goal.

Here's an example of how you could write your outcome goal:

- My puppy Roscoe is fully potty trained by December 1, 2018.

Notice how I didn't say Roscoe will be potty trained, I wrote it in the present tense as if Roscoe is already fully potty trained.

The difference is subtle but significant. You'll also notice that there's a date attached to the goal.

This is another very important aspect of setting goals that people often forget to do. Setting a date for when the goal will be accomplished by makes it real.

It's no longer something that you'll get around to eventually. Your mind now has a date and can work backwards from that date to start achieving it.

Finally, you want to make sure that you write your goals down and place them someplace where you'll see them regularly like your desk or a wall by your desk.

Writing down your goals and then hiding them will do you no good. Aside from outcome goals, there are also process goals.

These types of goals are important too. Process goals are the things you actually need to do in order to reach your outcome.

If you think of it like a mountain, the outcome goals are at the top of the mountain where you ultimately want to get to.

The process goals are the rest of the mountain and they'll tell you how to climb the mountain so you can get to where you want to go. Here are some examples of process goals that you could use for potty training:

- I take Roscoe outside to go potty every 2 hours.
- I tightly control Roscoe's environment in the house to the living room.
- I give Roscoe praise and a treat every time he uses the bathroom outside.

Setting process goals such as these will help to remind you of what it is that you need to do, and it'll keep you on track to achieving the outcome goal that you want!

# Conclusion

Potty training is a necessary part of owning a puppy. Sure it's not the most fun thing in the world, but it's rewarding to accomplish that goal with your puppy.

The journey will have ups and downs, but remember why it is you're doing this in the first place. Stick with it because in the end, it'll all be worth it!

These next few months of training your dog won't be the easiest, but once it's done, you'll have a well-trained dog for years to come. Thank you so much for reading this book to the end and I wish you the best of luck in potty training your puppy!

Made in the USA
Columbia, SC
24 February 2021

33484635R00081